Expert Learning
for
Law Students
Workbook

Expert Learning
for
Law Students
Workbook

SECOND EDITION

Michael Hunter Schwartz

WASHBURN UNIVERSITY SCHOOL OF LAW

CAROLINA ACADEMIC PRESS

Durham, North Carolina

ISBN 978-1-59460-552-9
LCCN 2008924393

CAROLINA ACADEMIC PRESS
700 Kent Street
Durham, North Carolina 27701
Telephone (919) 489-7486
Fax (919) 493-5668
www.cap-press.com

Printed in the United States of America

Contents

Expert Learning
for
Law Students
Workbook

Reflection Questions for Chapter 1

1. How are novice self-regulated learners different from expert self-regulated learners?

2. Why do self-regulated learners achieve higher grades than students who are not self-regulated learners?

3. In what ways do you already do things that expert self-regulated learners do? In what ways do you not?

Reflection Questions for Chapter 2

1. How will law school be different from your undergraduate or other graduate studies?

2. What particular challenges do you anticipate from the ways in which law students are tested?

3. Explain what it means to say learning in law school involves vicarious learning and self-teaching and what these two characteristics of law school learning demand of law students.

4. How will the differences between law school and your past educational experiences change how you will study and learn?

Reflection Questions for Chapter 3

1. Given your own experiences as a learner and what you have learned in this chapter, how do you learn? In other words, what aspects of Cognitivism and Constructivism are consistent with your own learning experiences and what aspects of your own learning cannot be explained by either of these learning theories?

2. How will what you have learned about Cognitivism influence how you study law?

3. How will what you have learned about Schema Theory influence how you study law?

4.   How will what you have learned about Constructivism influence how you study law?

Reflection Questions for Chapter 4

1. At various times in this chapter, as well as in Chapter 1, self-regulated learners are described as "proactive," "in control," "strategic," "consciously aware," "goal oriented" and "driven to rectify failure and to construct understanding." To what extent are these characterizations an outgrowth of engaging in the behaviors described as a part of the SRL cycle?

2. What aspects of the SRL cycle make sense to you? Why? What have you observed in your life as a student that makes you believe that these aspects will work for your law school studies? What aspects of the SRL cycle do not make sense to you? Why? What have you observed in your life as a student that makes you believe that these aspects will not work for your law school studies?

Exercise 5-1

The exercise reflected in the table below was designed to make sure you can correctly classify typical law school assignments. For each of the following excerpts from law school syllabi, classify each learning task implicated. For each of these excerpts, more than one learning task will be implicated.

Question No.	Course	Week	Topic(s)	Assignment	Learning Tasks Implicated (check each task implicated)
5-1.1	Contracts	Week 5	Damages for Breach of Contract	*Hawkins* (pp. 3–7); *Sullivan* (pp. 7–8); *Groves* (pp. 11–18); Peevyhouse (pp. 19–22); Johnson (pp. 22–25); Dix Construction (pp. 36–39)	☐ Reading Comprehension ☐ Research ☐ Synthesis ☐ Problem Solving ☐ Memorization ☐ Organization ☐ Concept Learning ☐ Principle Learning ☐ Legal Writing
5-1.2	Legal Research and Writing	Week 7	Objective Memorandum	Research the issues raised in the client letter distributed in class and prepare an objective memo analyzing the issues	☐ Reading Comprehension ☐ Research ☐ Synthesis ☐ Problem Solving ☐ Memorization ☐ Organization ☐ Concept Learning ☐ Principle Learning ☐ Legal Writing
5-1.3	Torts	Week 15	Final Examination	None	☐ Reading Comprehension ☐ Research ☐ Synthesis ☐ Problem Solving ☐ Memorization ☐ Organization ☐ Concept Learning ☐ Principle Learning ☐ Legal Writing

Exercise 5-2

This exercise is designed to help you develop your ability to invoke self-interest and self-efficacy. Select a course in which you are currently enrolled. If you are not enrolled in any course right now, answer the questions below with respect to this chapter of this book. You should force yourself to write at least one paragraph in response to each question.

5-2.1 Why do you want to become a lawyer?

5-2.2 Why are you interested in this subject matter?

5-2.3 How will you use what you are learning in this course when you become a lawyer? How will you use it in your current job (or how could you have used what you are learning in a past job)?

5-2.4 When and how have you succeeded in doing something similar to what you need to do to succeed in this course (try to think of something that, at the very least, is similar in terms of degree of difficulty and amount of work). (If you are really struggling to think of something, consider one of the following: learning to play a musical instrument, learning to cook, learning a sport or learning statistics, chemistry or calculus.)

Exercise 5-3

This exercise is designed to help you develop the skill of goal-setting. Respond to each of the questions and sub-questions below in writing.

5-3.1 Set a goal for some non-academic aspect of your life, such as an exercise goal, a healthy-eating goal, or a goal for your relationship with a significant other in your life.

_____

_____

_____

_____

Check your goal to see if it is a proper one; ask yourself:

Is the goal concrete? (A goal of finding one's inner self, while undoubtedly valuable, is not concrete because it lacks criteria for success and objective evidence of success whereas a goal of listing one's ten most important values is concrete.)

_____

_____

Is the goal short-term? (A goal of finding a spouse when you are not dating anyone at all is probably not short-term whereas a goal of participating in an activity in which you would meet other single people would be short-term.)

_____

_____

Is the goal challenging? (A goal of finding a list of job openings in your field would probably not be challenging, but a goal of applying for five jobs may be.)

_____

_____

Is the goal realistic? (A goal of mastering the sport of bowling when you have never bowled would not be realistic but a goal of learning the rules of the game and the basics of playing would be.)

_____

_____

5-3.2 Set a goal for learning the skill of goal-setting.

_____

_____

_____

_____

Check your goal to see if it is a proper one; ask yourself:

Is the goal concrete? (How will you know whether you have achieved the goal?)

_____

_____

Is the goal short-term? (Have you set a goal that you can achieve in a sort time frame?)

_____

_____

Is the goal challenging? (Will you find the learning intellectually challenging?)

_____

_____

Is the goal realistic? (Is it achievable?)

_____

_____

Exercise 5-4

This exercise focuses on developing your skills in selecting and using motivational strategies and environmental strategies. In the next chapter of this book, you will be reading and learning about your personality type and learning style and the implications of each for how you should study in law school. The task of reading Chapter 6 involves reading comprehension, concept learning and principle learning. For that chapter, respond to each of the items below in writing:

5-4.1   At what time of day and on what day will you study this material? Why did you select these days and times?

5-4.2   When will you take breaks? How will you space your studying? For how long will you take your breaks?

5-4.3   What will you do to *reward* yourself during your breaks or after you finish studying?

5-4.4   List three things you will say to yourself to keep focused while you are reading. At least one should be a list of steps you will follow as you read and at least one other should be a reference to a past success on a similar learning task.

5-4.5   Where will you study this material? Why did you select this location?

5-4.6   With whom will you study? Why did you select this (these) person(s)?

Reflection Questions for Chapter 5

1. How will you know what learning tasks in which you should be engaging?

2. Why are you going to law school?

3. What courses will you be taking in your first semester of law school? Find out if you do not already know. What do you find interesting about each subject? Determine the rough contours of what each course addresses (e.g., contract law deals with private disputes between parties relating to promises the courts deem enforceable) and then brainstorm reasons why that subject might interest you.

4.   Why is self-efficacy so highly correlated with student success? Can you think of a time when your self-efficacy influenced your results on a test, project or task?

5.   Why are effective learning goals concrete, short-term, challenging and realistic?

6.   Why does spaced study produce better learning than cramming?

7. What are the obstacles to your time management in law school? What will be are the keys to success in managing your time?

8. What motivational, environmental and cognitive strategies have been most effective in your past learning exercises?

Reflection Questions for Chapter 6

1. What is your four-letter personality type? How might your personality type influence how you go about studying law?

2. What is your learning style? How might your learning style influence how you go about studying law?

3. Throughout this text, you will find a number of lists of things, such as the steps involved in performing the forethought phase, the list of types of law school learning activities and the list of learning styles. For which personality types and learning styles have these lists been designed?

4.   You will also find many graphic images in this text. For which personality types and learning styles have these graphics been designed?

Exercise 7-1

This exercise focuses on developing your repertoire of techniques for focusing your attention while you are engaged in learning activities. It will also reinforce some of what you already have learned about self-regulated learning. The questions below will require you to perform in writing each of the five steps of the forethought phase of the SRL cycle for the materials you will be reading in Chapter 8. Thus, before you start to perform each step of the forethought phase, you will state out loud and in writing how you should do each step (a self-guiding verbalization) and, after you finish that step, you will articulate a statement praising yourself for completing that step (positive self-talk). If you need to do so, feel free to refer back to Chapter 5 as you work.

7-1.1 Forethought Step 1: Perceive the task

Self-guiding verbalization:

Performance:

Praise when finished:

7-1.2 Forethought Step 2: Classifying the task

Self-guiding verbalization:

Performance:

Praise when finished:

7-1.3 Forethought Step 3: Invoking self-interest and self-efficacy

Self-guiding verbalization:

Performance:

_____

_____

_____

_____

_____

_____

Praise when finished:

_____

_____

_____

_____

_____

_____

7-1.4 Forethought Step 4: Setting learning goals

Self-guiding verbalization:

_____

_____

_____

_____

_____

_____

_____

Performance:

_____

_____

_____

_____

_____

_____

Praise when finished:

_____

_____

_____

_____

_____

7-1.5 Forethought Step 5: Selecting strategies (including cognitive, motivational and environmental strategies)

Self-guiding verbalization:

_____

_____

_____

_____

_____

_____

_____

Performance:

_____

_____

_____

_____

_____

Praise when finished:

_____

_____

_____

_____

_____

_____

Exercise 7-2

This exercise focuses on developing your self-monitoring skills. Complete the time management/self-monitoring log on the back of this page for the materials in Chapter 8 of the book. To assist you in completing this exercise, I have labeled the four concepts addressed in Chapter 8. You will need to do most of the work on this exercise after you have completed Chapter 7 and are ready to begin studying Chapter 8.

Time Management/Self-Monitoring Log for Chapter 8

Concept/Skill to be Studied	Learning Goal(s)	Strategy(ies) for Learning	Place for Studying	Time Planned for Studying and for Breaks	Actual Study Time and Study Breaks	Actual Time Getting Help and Source of that Help	Ability to Focus During Study	Steps Used to Study the Material	How Effective Was My Study Technique
Self-Evaluation									
Attribution									
Self-Reaction									
Adaptation									

Reflection Questions for Chapter 7

1. For each of the four techniques for focusing attention, explain why that technique helps learners to focus their attention.

2. Why is self-monitoring so crucial for expert learning?

3. Recall a learning experience that did not go as well as you would have liked it to have gone. Was there a point in time before you received your grade when you knew things were not going well?

If your answer to the above question is "yes," how did you know? Why were you unable to address the issue(s) productively?

If your answer to the above question is "no," why do you think you were unaware that you were having a learning difficulty?

4.   Why is monitoring for help seeking so important to success in law school?

Exercise 8-1

This exercise focuses on developing your ability to self-evaluate your learning. Select a recent learning experience (in college, at work or your efforts to learn the materials in this text) and then answer each of the questions below in the space provided.

8-1.1 Did you master what you were supposed to learn? (Did you learn to do what you were supposed to learn to do? Did you develop an understanding of what you were supposed to understand?) (internal assessment)

Complete the following sentence: I was supposed to learn

_____

_____

_____

Circle the correct conclusion: I DID / DID NOT master what I was supposed to learn.

8-1.2 How well did you perform on any formal (a test or paper) or self-imposed (a practice test or trial run) assessment opportunity? (external assessment)

_____

_____

_____

8-1.3 Given your results, was your learning process as efficient as it should have been? Explain. (criteria-based assessment)

_____

_____

_____

8-1.4 How accurate was your internal assessment? (Did you accurately self-assess the extent to which you had mastered what you were supposed to learn?) Explain why you believe your internal evaluation was either accurate or inaccurate. (Why did you either correctly self-assess your degree of mastery or incorrectly self-assess your degree of mastery?) (reflective evaluation)

_____

_____

_____

_____

Exercise 8-2

This exercise focuses on developing your attribution skills. For this reason, you need to identify an instance in your life when you have *failed* (in college, at work or while reading this book) to learn something as well as you would have liked to have learned it and then respond to the questions below.

8-2.1   What was your failure to learn?

_____

_____

_____

8-2.2   Check each of the items below that reflect a cause of your failure to learn. The chart below is a slightly modified reproduction of Figure 9 in the book.

Possible problems in the Forethought Phase

☐ Failure to set appropriate goal (you set no goal or set improper one)
☐ Incorrect assessment of the learning task (you erroneously classified it)
☐ Failure to invoke self-efficacy (you failed to identify past success in similar learning enterprises)
☐ Failure to develop interest in the learning task (you did not determine why you were interested in learning the material)
☐ Poor motivational strategy choices (you could not stay motivated)
☐ Poor environmental choices (you made bad location, timing, rest choices)
☐ Poor cognitive strategy choices (your strategy choices proved unsuited to the task or the task required additional, unused strategies)

Possible problems in the Performance Phase

☐ Incorrect implementation of strategy choices (you incorrectly used the strategies)
☐ Failure to maintain focused attention (you were unable to focus during implementation)
☐ Failure to self-monitor (you failed to recognize a breakdown in the learning process while it was ongoing)
☐ Insufficient persistence (the task simply required multiple learning cycles)

Possible problems in the reflection phase

☐ Failure to pursue opportunities for self-assessment (student did not take advantage of or create opportunities for practice and feedback)
☐ Inaccurate self-assessment (you incorrectly assessed your success)

8-2.3   Review your answers to 8-2.1 and 8-2.2 above and then explain what you specifically did not do that you should have done or what you did incorrectly and why you committed the error(s).

_____

_____

_____

_____

Exercise 8-3

This exercise allows you to reflect upon past successes and failures in learning and how those successes and failures made you feel about yourself. Answer the questions below.

8-3.1 Identify a successful learning experience in the past. Select an experience that involved a significant amount of difficulty and/or hard work. How did your success make you feel about yourself? Do you feel any differently about that result based on what you have learned so far in this book?

_____

_____

_____

_____

_____

_____

_____

_____

_____

_____

_____

8-3.2 Now, identify an unsuccessful learning experience in your past. Choose the same experience as you chose for Exercise 8-2. How did your failure to learn make you feel about yourself? Do you feel any differently about that result based on what you have learned so far in this book?

_____

_____

_____

_____

_____

_____

_____

_____

Exercise 8-4

This exercise focuses on developing your ability to adapt your strategic approach in light of your learning goals, self-assessment and attributions. Review your answers to questions 8-2.1–8-2.3 and 8-3.2 and then answer the following questions.

8-4.1 In light of what you have learned so far from this text and your answers to questions 8-2.1 through 8-2.3, how could you modify the approach(es) you used to learn the material to make your learning process more successful and more efficient?

\
\
\
\
\
\
\
\
\
\
\
\

8-4.2 Explain why you are making the above adaptations by connecting the adaptations to your learning goal(s) and your self-evaluation of your learning. Be sure your adaptation is systematic by making only relatively small change(s) and by basing your changes on your self-evaluation and your goal.

\
\
\
\
\
\
\
\

Reflection Questions for Chapter 8

1. How does the reflection phase influence the forethought and the performance phases?

2. Many novice learners never engage in any of the behaviors described in this chapter. Why do novice learners avoid these behaviors?

3. Have you ever engaged in the behaviors described in this chapter? Describe what you did.

4.   In what sense is the reflection phase the most self-empowering phase of the SRL cycle?

Exercise 9-1

This exercise is an opportunity for you to practice your SRL and pre-reading skills with respect to two of the cases you will be reading in your first week of law school and to gain some insight into the benefits of using the pre-reading strategies you have learned in Chapter 9. Before you begin this exercise, select two cases you are required to read for your first week of law school classes. Then, **copy** the form below and answer the questions below for both cases.

<u>FORETHOUGHT PHASE</u>

9-1.1 What is my assignment?

_____

_____

_____

9-1.2 Classify the learning task.

What is the general subject area?

_____

What type(s) of task(s) are involved? (select all that apply)

☐ *Reading comprehension*   ☐ *Research*   ☐ *Synthesis>*
☐ *Problem-solving*   ☐ *Concept learning*   ☐ *Principle learning*

State the basis(es) for your classification(s).

_____

_____

_____

9-1.3 Invoking self-interest — What interests you about this assignment? (*Are you a person who enjoys all types of learning experiences? Are you interested in this particular subject? How might you use in other contexts what you will be learning from the cases?*)

_____

_____

_____

_____

_____

_____

9-1.4 Invoking self-efficacy — Why do you believe that you will succeed in learning this material? (*Have you successfully learned something similar [or at least something equally difficult-to-learn] in another educational setting? At work? At a musical instrument or a sport? Why did you succeed?*)

9-1.5 Setting learning goals — What do you wish to accomplish here? (*Remember the four criteria for learning goals: (1) They must be behavioral and state criteria for their accomplishment; (2) They must be short-term; (3) They must be challenging; (4) They must be realistic.*)

9-1.6. Selecting Learning Strategies

Motivational Strategies — What motivational strategies will you use? (e.g., rewards, self-talk)

What environmental strategies will you use?

Where will you study?

When will you study?

_____

_____

When will you take breaks?

_____

_____

_____

With whom will you study?

_____

_____

_____

Cognitive Strategies

What technique(s) will you use to study this material? (*Hint: There is only one right answer to this question.*)

_____

_____

PERFORMANCE PHASE

9-1.7 Attention-focusing: How will you remain focused on your learning task?

_____

_____

_____

_____

_____

_____

_____

9-1.8. Self-monitoring: Remember to self-monitor for comprehension, efficiency, efficacy of environmental strategy selections, help-seeking and attention.

9-1.9. (Implementation starts here) In what sense do judges create meaning with their opinions?

_____

_____

9-1.10 In what sense do you create meaning when you read an opinion?

9-1.11 Develop knowledge about the general subject of case(s). (*Hint: You are looking for information about the relationships among the topics in the course and, in particular, among the topics you are learning. Consider drawing a chart to depict those relationships.*)

What information about this subject can you infer from the syllabus?

What information about this subject can you infer from the text's table of contents?

Look at a hornbook addressing the course. (Most law libraries have hornbooks on reserve.) What information about this subject can you infer from the hornbook's table of contents?

Draw a chart to depict the relationships you have identified.

9-1.12 Read the introduction to the chapter (if there is one). What did you learn from that introduction that is relevant to the particular subject area you are now studying?

_____

_____

_____

_____

_____

_____

_____

9-1.13 Read the questions and comments after the case(s). (*Hint: Sometimes the relevant questions and comments are placed after a following cases or cases.*)

What have you learned from the questions and comments? (*Hint: The questions and comments often provide insights into what is important about the case.*)

_____

_____

_____

_____

_____

_____

_____

_____

9-1.14 Read a hornbook section addressing the topic. What have you learned about the topic from the hornbook?

_____

_____

_____

_____

_____

_____

9-1.15 Preview the case(s) by reading the headings and the first sentence of each paragraph of each case. What do you now know about the case(s)?

9-1.16 List the following details:

The court:

Do you know anything relevant about this court?

The judge:

Do you know anything relevant about this judge?

The date of the opinion:

Do you know anything about this time in history?

The state:

Do you know anything about the politics of this state or its reputation for legal innovation?

The Citation:

9-1.17 Generating questions: Create at least 10 questions about the case you are about to read. (Note: no more than two questions should be memory-type questions and no more than four should be comprehension think-type questions)

1.

2.

3.

4.

5.

6.

7.

8.

9.

10.

REFLECTION PHASE

9-1.18 How well did you understand what to expect and look for when you read the case?

9-1.19 What factors best explain your success or failure in understanding what to expect and look for when you read the case? (if you feel you failed to understand, see Chapter 8 for the list of possible causes of failures to learn)

9-1.20 How do you feel about your success or failure in understanding what to expect and look for when you read the case? How do these results compare to your results on similar assignments you have had in the past?

9-1.21 How will you change your approach to pre-reading to achieve a higher level of success in future pre-reading efforts? (Answer this question even if you feel you succeeded in understanding what to expect and look for when you read the case.)

Exercise 9-2

This exercise is an opportunity for you to practice your reading skills with respect to one of the cases you will be reading in your first week of law school and to gain some insight into the benefits of using the reading strategies you have learned in Chapter 9. For this exercise, use the two cases you selected for exercise 9-1 above. **Copy** the form below and fill it out for both cases.

9-2.1 You need to make sure you monitor your learning for comprehension. Students who are just learning how to read court opinions almost always struggle a lot. Accordingly, in the space below and as you read the opinion, identify at least three places in the opinion that you (at least initially) found confusing.

    1.

    2.

    3.

9-2.2 Review your ten questions from question 9-1.17 above. Answer at least five of those questions in the space below (be sure to indicate in some way which questions you are answering).

    1.

    2.

    3.

4. _____

5. _____

9-2.3 In the space provided, develop at least one graphic depiction of the facts of the case.

9-2.4 Expert law students critique courts' reasoning and assertions. In the space provided below, record your disagreement or critique of at least two aspects of the court's opinion. (Keep in mind that every opinion you read raised a close enough question that the court chose to publish the opinion to clarify the law. Also, try asking yourself the following questions as you read each sentence: Do I agree with this statement? Why or why not? What must the lawyer for the party who lost in this court have argued? What aspect of that lawyer's argument seems more persuasive than the court's argument? How might a future lawyer interpret this case in a way the court never intended? What could the court have decided instead? Why might that alternative be an improvement over what the court said?)

9-2.5 You also should be coming up with additional questions about the material as you read. Record at least three additional questions (and answers to those questions) in the spaces below.

1.

2.

3.

9-2.6 Finally, while reading for the big picture is most important, many new law students find it helpful to also attend to the details because the details help them acquire and master the new vocabulary they are learning. If you are a student who needs to focus on the big picture, skip this exercise. If, however, you benefit from also understanding the details and adopting the language, read the opinion on a word-by-word, line-by-line basis and complete this exercise. In the spaces below, list 20 words in the opinion you needed to look up in a law dictionary and the definition you found to be most applicable to the context in which you found the word.

Word

Definition

Word

Definition

Word

Definition

Word

Definition

Word

Definition

Word

Definition

Word

Definition

Word

Definition

Word

Definition

Word

Definition

Word

Definition

Word

Definition

Word

Definition

Word

Definition

Word

Definition

Word

Definition

Word

Definition

Word

Definition

Word

Definition

Word

Definition

Exercise 9-3

This exercise is an opportunity for you to practice your case briefing skills with respect to the two cases you used the pre-reading and reading strategies in Exercise 9-1. Copy and then complete the briefing form below for both cases:

Facts:

<u>Operative Facts</u>: (*State each fact upon which the court relied in making its decision and any other facts necessary to follow the court's reasoning.*)

<u>Procedural Facts</u>: (*What happened in the courts?*)

Issue:

<u>When</u> (*A-identify the character*)

<u>Does</u> (*B-identify the situation*)

<u>To</u> (*C-identify the recipient, if any*)

59

<u>What</u> (*D-identify the possible outcome*) <u>happens</u>?

Holding:

<u>When</u> (*A-identify the character in terms of status*)

<u>Does</u> (*B-identify the situation in general terms*)

<u>To</u> (*C-identify the recipient, **if any**, in general terms*)

<u>What</u> (*D-identify the outcome-what did the judge decide*) <u>happens</u>?

Rationale:

<u>Rule</u> (*State and paraphrase it*)

As stated by the Court:

Paraphrase:

Application (*Explain what the court said in applying the rule to the facts or in applying and/or distinguishing precedent to the facts*)

_____

_____

_____

_____

Public Policy (*Explain the reasons underlying the court's decision and all possible contrary policies*)

_____

_____

_____

_____

Synthesis (*How can this case be reconciled with the cases preceding and following it?*)

_____

_____

_____

_____

_____

_____

_____

_____

Dissenting and Concurring Opinions (*Summarize the argument(s) made in any dissenting or concurring opinion(s)*)

_____

_____

_____

_____

_____

_____

_____

_____

Reflection Questions for Chapter 9

1. How are pre-reading and reading strategies with respect to court opinions similar to strategies that would also be effective for reading non-law school texts? How are they different?

2. Which of the pre-reading and reading strategies identified in this chapter is new to you? Of those, which would have helped you as an undergraduate student? With which of the pre-reading and reading strategies identified in this chapter were you already familiar?

3. Why do law students who use the strategies detailed in this chapter get better grades than those who do not?

4.   Select three of the pre-reading or reading strategies and explain why you believe those strategies help students understand cases better.

5.   What does it mean to say expert learners "dialogue" with court opinions? Why does this strategy enhance comprehension and recall?

6.   Why do many lawyers continue to brief cases even after they graduate from law school?

7.   Based on your reading so far and what you know so far about lawyering, if you were a law professor, would you prefer detailed issue statements or detailed holdings or both? Why?

8.   Some students mistakenly believe that policy is really irrelevant, in part because many courts do not explicitly state the policy rationales for their decisions. Why are these students mistaken?

9.   Why do expert learners state rules in two different ways?

10.   What is the benefit of synthesizing cases?

Exercise 10-1

This exercise will allow you to self-test your developing classroom learning skills. For your first law school class, use the classroom learning skills described in this chapter. Specifically, in addition to carefully reading and briefing the cases and using the strategies described in the chapter, make sure your notes use the two-thirds/one-third format, use plenty of good abbreviations and have an outline-like structure. After class, exchange notes with a friend in the class or with the other members of a study group and discuss your classroom learning activities with your friend or study group. Then, have your friend or group critique your efforts by placing a check mark next to each activity described below. (The chart below is a slightly-modified reproduction of Figure 30 in the book.)

Class Preparation Activities

- ☐ Set explicit, mastery learning goal
- ☐ Read and brief all assigned cases
- ☐ Review and synthesize notes from previous class session
- ☐ Plan notes
- ☐ Plan attention-focusing strategies
- ☐ Assume disagreement with some aspect of the classroom discussion
- ☐ Develop list of questions and areas of confusion

Effective Listening

- ☐ Prepare for class as above
- ☐ Ready yourself mentally (remove distractions, avoid hasty judgments, boredom, frustration and anger and be physically ready)
- ☐ Self-monitor as you listen (see Chapter 7)
- ☐ Actively listen by striving to make sense of everything you hear

Effective Note-Taking

- ☐ Focus on key points and follow instructional cues
- ☐ Leave lots of space for notes
- ☐ Correct confusion and restate understanding in own words
- ☐ Organize as you go

Post-Class Activities

- ☐ Review for comprehension and legibility
- ☐ Reflect on classroom learning experience
- ☐ Transfer to course outline and graphic organizer(s)

Reflection Questions for Chapter 10

1. Why does it help students learn better if they plan the structure of their notes and force their notes to fit an outline-like (hierarchical) format?

2. Why do lawyers use the two-thirds/one-third approach to note-taking during depositions and trials?

3. How have you prepared for class in the past? Why might the strategies described in this chapter help you to learn more and to learn it better?

Exercise 11-1

This exercise is a tool for creating a successful cooperative learning group from the outset. It has been designed to allow each member of your study group to understand everyone else's expectations for and obligations to the group. Make enough copies of the questions below so that each member of your study group can fill out this form.

11-1.1 Why are you in a cooperative learning group? What do you expect to gain from the experience?

_____

_____

_____

_____

11-1.2 Complete the following sentence: I will manifest my commitment to my fellow group members' law school success by . . .

_____

_____

_____

_____

11-1.3 Complete the following sentence: I believe group members who fail to adequately prepare for or attend a group meeting should have to . . .

_____

_____

_____

_____

11-1.4 In the space below, list three things that you believe to be keys to effective communication within your group. (*What do you want from your fellow group members in terms of communication? Support? Honesty? Willingness to give harsh feedback when necessary? Openness to hearing harsh feedback? Willingness to admit errors? Open-mindedness?*)

1. _____

_____

2. _____

_____

3.

11-1.5   Exchange your answers to questions 11-1.1 through 11-1.4 with the other members of your group and then fill in the form contract on the next page. Make sure each member of the group initials each paragraph in the spaces provided and signs the contract where indicated.

A SIMPLE, TWO-PAGE STUDY GROUP CONTRACT

1. **Commitment to Group Success.** Each member of this group hereby commits to working towards the law school success of every other member of the group. We will manifest this commitment in the following ways:

   1.1 _____

   _____

   1.2 _____

   _____

   1.3 _____

   _____

Initials: ____ ____ ____ ____ ____ ____

2. **Commitment to Preparation for Group Meetings.** Each member of this group commits to being personally responsible for preparing for each group session and holding everyone else in the group accountable for preparing for each group session.

   Preparation for each session will consist of: (*Note: you may simply say that group members must do whatever learning activity(ies) the group assigned itself at the previous group session.*)

   _____

   _____

   _____

   A group member will be deemed unprepared for a group session if: (*state a standard for making this determination, such as lack of written evidence that the group member has done the work or vote of the other members of the group*)

   _____

   _____

   _____

   A group member deemed unprepared for ____ group session(s) must:

   _____

   _____

   _____

A group member deemed unprepared for ___ group session(s) will be removed from the group.

Initials: ____   ____   ____   ____   ____   ____

3.   **Commitment to Group Communication.** Each group member hereby commits to the following communication goals for group meetings:

Goal 1: _____

_____

Goal 2: _____

_____

Goal 3: _____

_____

Goal 4: _____

_____

Goal 5: _____

_____

Initials: ____   ____   ____   ____   ____   ____

4.   **Signatures.** By signing this agreement, each member commits herself or himself to the terms listed above.

_____   _____

_____   _____

_____   _____

Reflection Questions for Chapter 11

1. The strategies for obtaining help addressed in this chapter are offered in a conscious order, the order that the author believes students should follow in seeking help. Why is this order probably the optimal one?

2. Why are study groups such a powerful learning tool?

3. Why are positive interdependence, promotive interaction, individual accountability, reflection on the group process and interpersonal and group skills so important to the success of cooperative learning groups?

Exercise 12-1

This exercise gives you an opportunity to practice deconstructing rules. For each of the rules below, deconstruct the rule into the correct number of parts and identify the type of rule it is.

12-1.1 Murder is the unlawful killing of another human being with malice aforethought.

Type of rule:

_____

Parts (H*int — there are five parts*):

_____

_____

_____

_____

_____

12-1.2 Unless otherwise unambiguously indicated, an offer to make a contract shall be construed as inviting acceptance in any manner.

Type of rule:

_____

Parts (*hint — there are two parts*):

_____

_____

_____

_____

12-1.3 A party has committed the tort of assault where the party causes another person to suffer an apprehension of an imminent battery.

Type of rule:

_____

Parts (*hint — there are six parts*):

_____

_____

_____

12-1.4 In deciding whether to issue an injunction before a trial on the merits, courts weigh way the benefit to the party requesting the injunction, the harm to the party opposing the injunction if the injunction were granted, the likelihood the party requesting the injunction will win at trial, and the interests of the general public.

Type of rule:

Parts (*hint — there are four parts*):

Exercise 12-2

This exercise provides you an opportunity to begin creating your first course outline. After you have completed your first major topic or sub-topic in one of your courses (such as intentional torts in your torts class, consideration in your contracts course, subject matter jurisdiction in your civil procedure course, estates in your property course, or mens rea in your criminal law course), **outline that topic**. Try doing your outline on a computer so that you can easily modify it as you work. After you finish your outline, use the following checklist to self-evaluate your outline or exchange outlines with a peer and use the checklist to evaluate your peer's outline.

Checklist for Outline Evaluation

☐ Was the outline completed shortly after the class finished the topic reflected in the outline?

☐ Does the outline adapt traditional outlining conventions (i.e., at least a II for every I, a B for every A, a 2 for every 1, etc.)?

☐ Does the outline reflect an effort to create structure? (Are there topics, sub-topics and sub-sub-topics, etc.?)

☐ Does the outline reflect what the professor has indicated is important?

☐ Does it include all the rules learned?

☐ Does it include holdings for each of the cases?

☐ Does it include examples and non-examples of each concept?

☐ Does it identify the public policy implications of the rules and holdings?

Exercise 12-3

This exercise allows you to try creating two of the various types of graphic organizers that law students use to organize what they have learned. Select a different subject area than the one you selected for Exercise 12-2 and create two different types of graphic organizers to depict the information. Feel free to look at the materials in Chapter 12 if you need help remembering the steps involved in creating any of the graphic organizers addressed in the chapter.

Reflection Questions for Chapter 12

1. Why is it helpful for law students to deconstruct rules? Why do students also need to be able to identify what type of rule each particular rule is?

2. Have you ever created a course outline? For what course? Did it help you learn the course material? Did you violate any of the principles for creating an effective outline?

3. Have you ever created a graphic organizer? Which type? For what course? Did it help you learn the course material?

4.   Based on what you have learned in this book about personality types and learning styles, who would you expect to benefit from creating graphic organizers? Why? Why might all law students benefit from creating graphic organizers?

5.   Answer this question after you have completed Exercises 12-2 and 12-3. Of the strategies you tried in Exercises 12-2 and 12-3, which strategy worked best for you? Why?

Exercise 13-1

This exercise allows you to practice connecting the new things you are learning in law school to things you learned before you went to law school. It also allows you to connect things you are learning in each of your law school courses to things you are learning in your other law school courses. Answer each of the questions below.

13-1.1 Identify two different concepts you have learned so far in your law school courses that are similar to two concepts you learned before you went to law school. Explain the ways in which the concepts are similar.

Law school concept:

_____

Similar pre-law school concept:

_____

How are the above two concepts similar?

_____

_____

Law school concept:

_____

Similar pre-law school concept:

_____

How are the above two concepts similar?

_____

_____

13-1.2 Identify two different concepts you have learned so far in one law school course that are similar to two concepts you learned in another law school course. (*For example, the concepts of intent in criminal law and in tort law are very similar.*)

Law school concept:

_____

Other law school concept:

_____

How are the above two concepts similar?

_____

_____

Law school concept:

_____

Other law school concept:

_____

How are the above two concepts similar?

_____

_____

_____

Exercise 13-2

This exercise allows you to practice using two of the six associational techniques you learned in Chapter 13 (imagery, analogies and the four types of mnemonics) to memorize materials you need to be memorizing for two of your first-year courses: contracts and criminal law.

13-2.1 An offer of a contract creates a power in the recipient of the offer (known as "the offeree") to form a contract by accepting. However, that power to accept may be lost *("terminated") by any of the following: a revocation, a counter-offer, a rejection, death of the offeror or offeree, incapacity of the offeror or the offeree, or lapse of time.*

Use an associational technique to memorize the italicized portion of the rule above by answering the questions below.

Technique

_____

Image, analogy or mnemonic

_____

_____

_____

_____

_____

13-2.2 *Larceny is the taking and carrying away of the personal property of another with intent to steal.*

Use an associational technique to memorize the rule above by answering the questions below.

Technique

_____

Image, analogy or mnemonic

_____

_____

_____

_____

_____

Exercise 13-3

This exercise allows you to practice one of the rehearsal techniques you learned in Chapter 13, flashcards, to memorize materials you need to be memorizing for one of your first-year courses, torts. After your class has completed its study of intentional torts, make a flashcard for each element of each of the intentional torts or your holdings for each of the cases you have read that deals with an intentional torts issue. Review your flash-cards with a partner until you can correctly state what is on the back of each card by only seeing the front of the card.

Exercise 13-4

This exercise allows you to practice paraphrasing rules and holdings. Select three rules or case holdings you have identified or developed so far in law school. Try to select rules or holdings from at least two different courses and include at least one rule and one holding. Then, answer the questions below.

13-4.1 Rule/holding number one.

State the rule/holding as it is phrased by a court, statute or restatement

Restate the rule/holding in your own words

Is your paraphrase accurate? How do you know? (*Consider testing your paraphrase against cases or asking your professor or a peer.*)

13-4.2 Rule/holding number two.

State the rule/holding as it is phrased by a court, statute or restatement

Restate the rule/holding in your own words

Is your paraphrase accurate? How do you know? (*Consider testing your paraphrase against cases or asking your professor or a peer.*)

13-4.3 Rule/holding number three.

State the rule/holding as it is phrased by a court, statute or restatement

Restate the rule/holding in your own words

Is your paraphrase accurate? How do you know? (*Consider testing your paraphrase against cases or asking your professor or a peer.*)

Exercise 13-5

This exercise allows you to practice developing examples and non-examples of law school concepts. For each of the concepts below, create an example and a non-example of that concept and explain your answers in the space provided. Generate your examples and non-examples from your own imagination; do not simply copy the facts of one of the cases you have read or a professor's hypothetical.

13-5.1 The tort of battery.

Example

_____

_____

Explanation of example

_____

_____

_____

_____

Non-Example

_____

_____

Explanation of non-example

_____

_____

_____

_____

_____

13-5.2 Offer in contract law.

Example

_____

_____

Explanation of example

_____

_____

_____

Non-Example

Explanation of non-example

13-5.3 A situation where a party has had sufficient contact with the forum state for a court in that state to assert personal jurisdiction over the defendant.

Example

Explanation of example

Non-Example

Explanation of non-example

Reflection Questions for Chapter 13

1. Why is memorization crucial to success in law school? Why isn't memorization sufficient to succeed in law school?

2. What is the relationship between the organizational strategies you learned in Chapter 12 and memorization?

3. How does clustering facilitate memorization?

4.   For what types of students is imagery a particularly powerful learning tool?

5.   Why are mnemonics and rehearsal less favored memorization techniques?

6.   Why are paraphrasing and generating examples and non-examples effective memorization tools?

7.   Answer this question only after you have completed Exercises 12-1 and 13-1 to 13-5. Now that you have tried each of the memorizations strategies described in this chapter, you can begin evaluating which of the techniques work best for you. Rank the techniques in order of your preference for using that technique. Explain your rankings.

Rankings

1.

2.

3.

4.

5.

6.

Explanation of Rankings

Exercise 14-1

This exercise gives you an opportunity to practice translating research procedures into checklists. Below is a simplified procedure for finding cases on a particular point. In the space provided, convert the steps into a checklist you can use while you are looking for cases.

1. STEP 1: Brainstorm a list of words and short phrases describing the situation for which you are looking for a case. Consider as possibilities abstract descriptions of your factual situation or basic principles or areas of law that you suspect apply.

2. STEP 2: Determine the jurisdiction in which the events in question took place.

3. STEP 3: Find the case digest (the index) for the jurisdiction and look for the words and phrases you have brainstormed. If you find the words with a case or a set of cases listed next to them, list all the cases and go to the volume in which each appears and get that case.

4. STEP 4: If you cannot find any of the words and phrases you brainstormed, brainstorm additional words and short phrases and then repeat step 3 above.

5. STEP 5: If, after performing step 4 above, you still cannot find a case, look for the words and phrases in a treatise or other secondary source (which may either list applicable cases or, at least, suggest additional words and phrases you might look for in the digest).

6. STEP 6: If you still have not found a case, your search is flawed or there is no case on point.

A Simple Case-Finding Checklist

Exercise 14-2

This exercise allows you to try out the research log in Figure 42 of the text. Complete the log below for your first few law school research assignments.

Research Topic[1]	Strategy Used[2]	Time[3]	Initial Result[4]	Final Result[5]

---

1. Write the specific subject/issue you are researching. Make sure you write the subject/issue each time because, as you research and become more expert in the subject, you will be refining your understanding of the topic.

2. List separately each specific strategy, including the specific resource (e.g., AmJur, Witkin) you are using. Be sure to list each strategy on its own line so you will later be able to evaluate its effectiveness. Note that, for each research project, you will need to use multiple strategies. For example, you often may start by reading a treatise to gain background insight into the subject and to identify the most significant cases in the general subject area before you look for statutes or case on point in a code or case index.

3. Record the amount of time you spent on this approach.

4. State your initial impressions of whether your approach was successful. Did you find what you were trying to find?

5. Indicate whether you have found everything you were supposed to have found, what you did not find (if anything), and why your approach either succeeded or did not succeed.

Exercise 14-3

This exercise focuses on helping you plan your paper-writing process. Below are a calendar and a list of activities typically required for first-semester legal writing papers and space for you to add additional activities required by your particular legal writing professor. Schedule each of the activities by writing on the calendar below and working backwards from the due date of the assignment to the date on which you received the assignment. Fill in the appropriate dates in the boxes in the upper left hand corner.

Sunday	Monday	Tuesday	Wednesday	Thursday	Friday	Saturday

Activities Checklist

- ☐ Analyze assignment and required tasks
- ☐ Plan calendar for project
- ☐ Brainstorm
- ☐ Plan research
- ☐ Begin research
- ☐ Finish research

- ☐ Sheppardize
- ☐ Organize paper
- ☐ Write first draft
- ☐ Edit first draft
- ☐ Perform follow-up research
- ☐ Write second draft
- ☐ Edit second draft

- ☐ Write third draft
- ☐ Check and revise citations
- ☐ _____
- ☐ _____
- ☐ _____
- ☐ _____

Exercise 14-4

Exercise 14-4 provides practice in editing your own work. Use this exercise to make sure you carefully edit your first legal writing paper. Respond to each of the questions below in the space provided.

14-4.1 Have you addressed all the issues and answered all the questions? ☐ Yes ☐ No

List the issues and questions in the directions.

_____

_____

14-4.2 Have you complied with all the formatting (i.e., font, page length, headings, margins, etc.) requirements? ☐ Yes ☐ No

List the formatting requirements for the assignment.

_____

_____

14-4.3 Have you either used all the information provided or made conscious choices not to use certain information? ☐ Yes ☐ No

List each piece of information you did not use and why you did not use it.

Info not used:

_____

Reason for not using it:

_____

Info not used:

_____

Reason for not using it:

_____

Info not used:

_____

Reason for not using it:

_____

Info not used:

_____

Reason for not using it:

_____

_____

14-4.4 Did you follow the organization you planned to follow? ☐ Yes ☐ No

If not, why not?

_____

_____

14-4.5 For each legal point you made, make sure you included every step of your reasoning. List each point in the space provided. Then, confirm that you actually did include every step of your reasoning in your discussion of that point and place a check mark in the box next to that point if you did include every step of your reasoning.

☐ _____

☐ _____

☐ _____

☐ _____

☐ _____

☐ _____

☐ _____

☐ _____

☐ _____

☐ _____

☐ _____

☐ _____

☐ _____

☐ _____

☐ _____

☐ _____

☐ _____

☐ _____

☐ _____

14-4.6   List every important authority on which you relied in your analysis. Then, confirm that you discussed that authority in appropriate depth and place a check mark in the space next to that authority if you discussed that authority in depth.

☐ _____

☐ _____

☐ _____

☐ _____

☐ _____

☐ _____

☐ _____

☐ _____

☐ _____

☐ _____

☐ _____

☐ _____

☐ _____

☐ _____

14-4.7   Did you check for typos? ☐ Yes ☐ No

14-4.8   Did you grammar-check, spell-check and "think-check" your paper? ("Think-check" refers to looking for errors that spell-checkers and grammar-checkers do not catch.) ☐ Yes ☐ No

14-4.9   Are all of your sentences complete sentences and not run-ons? ☐ Yes ☐ No

14-4.10 Have you avoided the use of jargon? ☐ Yes ☐ No

14-4.11 Is your punctuation correct? ☐ Yes ☐ No

14-4.12 Did you use words properly? ☐ Yes ☐ No

14-4.13 Are your sentences parallel? ☐ Yes ☐ No

14-4.14 Are your pronoun references proper? ☐ Yes ☐ No

14-4.15 Do your verbs and subjects agree? ☐ Yes ☐ No

14-4.16 Does your sentence structure vary? ☐ Yes ☐ No

14-4.17 Is your writing interesting? ☐ Yes ☐ No

14-4.18 Does the paper flow logically? Is it easy to read? Are there good transitions between ideas, sentences and paragraphs? ☐ Yes ☐ No

14-4.19 Do you avoid falling into writing patterns, such as overusing semi-colons, certain phrases, certain words? ☐ Yes ☐ No

14-4.20 Do you avoid using meaningless words like "certainly" and "obviously"? ☐ Yes ☐ No

14-4.21 Is your writing overly cute? ☐ Yes ☐ No Sufficiently formal? ☐ Yes ☐ No

14-4.22 Is your citation form proper? Have you properly used abbreviations, commas, parentheses, fonts (e.g., italic font, underlined font)? ☐ Yes ☐ No

14-4.23 Do you provide authority for every assertion of law in the paper? ☐ Yes ☐ No For every assertion of fact? ☐ Yes ☐ No

14-4.24 Do you place quotation marks around every statement that is not your own? ☐ Yes ☐ No

Reflection Questions for Chapter 14

1. Why do expert law students keep a research log?

2. Why is time management a crucial factor for success on legal writing assignments?

3. What should students learn from the instructions for their legal writing assignments? How do expert law students use those instructions?

4.   Why do expert law students organize their papers before, during and after writing them?

5.   Why is reflection crucial to success on legal writing papers?

6.   Why is good basic writing a part of students' grades in legal writing courses? (*Hint: Consider who will be reading your legal writing once you start practicing law.*)

Exercise 15-1

This exercise has been designed to make sure you get the practice and feedback you need to begin developing the skill of spotting issues. For each subject you are taking, find at least three past examinations for which you can find model answers (see Chapter 15 for suggestions as to where you can find practice exam questions and answers). For each exam, complete the form below. In other words, if you are taking four doctrinal courses, you will need to make 12 copies of this form.

15-1.1 List all the issues, sub-issues and sub-sub-issues you believe are raised by the facts in the examination hypothetical.

1. _____

2. _____

3. _____

4. _____

5. _____

6. _____

7. _____

8. _____

9. _____

10. _____

15-1.2 Review the model answer to the hypothetical and compare the issues identified in the model answer with your list of issues in your answer to Question 15-1.1.

Which of the issues identified in your answer to 15-1.1 were correct?

☐ Issue 1   ☐ Issue 2   ☐ Issue 3   ☐ Issue 4   ☐ Issue 5

☐ Issue 6   ☐ Issue 7   ☐ Issue 8   ☐ Issue 9   ☐ Issue 10

15-1.3 For each issue you correctly identified as an issue, explain why that issue was raised by the facts.

_____

_____

_____

_____

_____

_____

_____

_____

_____

15-1.4 For each issue you incorrectly identified as an issue, explain why you believed it was an issue and why it was not actually an issue.

15-1.5 For each issue you discussed in your response to Question 15-1.4, explain how you will avoid making the same error in the future.

Exercise 15-2

This exercise is a small, first step towards developing your skills in applying rules to facts. In this exercise, you will read a series of hypothetical questions that raise a material fact issue (the legal issue analyzed in Figure 50 in Chapter 15) and then will respond to a series of questions that require you to work through the steps of applying rules to facts.

The first problem (15-2.1) is a hypothetical question followed by a model answer. Your only task is to read the question and the answer. Please note that this hypothetical has been designed to allow students to argue on behalf of both of the parties (because the question has no clear, correct answer as to how a court would decide the case). **The model answer includes comments and references to the Four Steps of Applying Rules to Facts.**

For the next few problems, the questions will guide you through the reasoning. Later questions will provide less guidance, and the last question will require you to supply all of the steps on your own. Use the "Four Steps of Applying Rules to Facts" (Figure 47) as you work all of these problems.

15-2.1 Larry Landowner was negotiating with Betty Buyer for Betty to buy, for $50,000, Purpleacre, a tract of farmland on which a corn crop is growing. Betty, who owns a chain of ice skating rinks, was planning to use the land to open an ice skating rink. During negotiations, Betty told Larry that her big concern was that the tract only was large enough for the rink and 40 parking spaces and that her ten other rinks had an average of 60 spaces. Larry then falsely told Betty that the person who owned a small neighboring tract had told Larry that he was willing to sell that tract for a good price. Betty thereafter agreed to buy the land from Larry. Three weeks before the sale was to close, Betty learned that the owner of the neighboring tract had never told anyone that he wanted to sell the small tract and, actually, was unwilling to sell at any price. Betty therefore refused to close the deal. Larry sued Betty for breach of contract. Is the fact that Larry misrepresented material so that Betty would not be likely to be held liable for breach?

Answer (with comments in parentheses): The question is whether the fact misrepresented by Larry was a material fact (**ID of issue**). A material fact, according to the majority rule, is a fact a reasonable person would consider important in deciding to enter into the contract (**Step 1 — statement of relevant rule**). In this case, Betty owned a chain of ice skating rinks and therefore was purchasing Purpleacre for $50,000 solely for the purpose of developing an ice skating rink. Betty determined the property was large enough for 40 parking spaces. Betty's other skating rinks, however, have an average of 60 spaces, and Larry falsely represented that the person who owned a small neighboring tract had told Larry that he was willing to sell that tract for a good price, when, in fact the owner of the tract is not willing to sell at any price. (**Steps 2–3 identify and state relevant facts**). On the one hand (note the signal, by these words, that arguments on two sides of the issue will be forthcoming), 40 parking spaces are one-third fewer than the average for Betty's rinks. One-third fewer spaces means one-third fewer customers will be able to park in the lot, and, therefore, pay to use the rink, which may cause Betty to earn less income from the rink, and income is a goal for any persons interested in using the land for business purposes. (**Step 4, Part 1A: Draw relevant and reasonable inferences from facts**). For this reason, a careful businessperson in Betty's situation arguably would regard the represented fact as significant at all in deciding whether to buy the property (**Step 4, Part 2A: Link inference to requirement of rule by using a synonym that references the key facts for the key requirement of the rule**).

113

On the other hand, the facts state that 60 spaces is the average for Betty's skating rinks, meaning that some of her rinks must have somewhat fewer spaces. Moreover, at least initially, it is unlikely Betty's rink will be full, and there are no facts suggesting that a rink with fewer spaces could not do as well as Betty's other rinks (note the pointing out of missing information). In fact, there is no fact suggesting there is no street parking available nearby (again note the pointing out of missing information). In addition, Betty will save money in not having to acquire the other lot. (**Step 4, Part 1B: Draw relevant and reasonable inferences from facts**). For these reasons, unless a rink with fewer spaces would not do well and there is no available street parking, a prudent business person arguably would not regard the misrepresented fact as a significant one in deciding to buy the property (**Step 4, Part 2B: Link inference to requirement of rule by using a synonym that references the key facts for the key requirement of the rule**).

Although the question is a close one, on balance, it seems more likely than not that a prudent businessperson in Betty's situation would rather purchase a lot with one-third more space for parking than a lot with one-third less parking. (**Step 4, Part C: Draw relevant and reasonable inference from fact and connect inference to requirement of rule by using a synonym that references the key facts for the key requirement of the rule**). Accordingly, because a reasonable person would regard the parking issue as an important fact in deciding whether to make the contract, the fact is a material fact (conclusion drawn in the language of the key requirement of the rule).

15-2.2   Larry Landowner was negotiating with Betty Buyer for Betty to buy, for $50,000, Purpleacre, a tract of farmland on which a corn crop is growing. Betty, who owns a chain of ice skating rinks, was planning to use the land to open an ice skating rink. During negotiations, Larry falsely told Betty that, within two years, Larry was planning to build a shopping mall on a nearby tract of land that Larry owned. Betty thereafter agreed to buy the land from Larry. Three weeks before the sale was to close, Betty discovered Larry never had any such in intention; in fact, Larry had promised the city council that he would not develop the other tract of land at all for the next fifteen years. Betty therefore refused to close the deal. Larry sued Betty for breach of contract. Is the fact that Larry misrepresented material so that Betty would not be likely to be held liable for breach?

Answer: The question is whether the fact misrepresented by Larry was a material fact (**identification of the issue**).

Step 1: *Identify and state the applicable rule of law.* A material fact, according to the majority rule, is a fact a reasonable person would consider important in deciding to enter into the contract.

Step 2: *Identify and list all facts that tend to prove or disprove the required state of facts described in the rule. (Reminder: Here, the required state of facts is that the misrepresented fact be one that a reasonable person in Betty's situation would consider important in deciding whether to purchase Purpleacre.)*

1. *(Hint: Betty's plans for the land)*

_____

2. *(Hint: The fact Larry misrepresented)*

_____

Step 3: *State (in writing) one factor one set of facts that tends to prove or disprove the existence of the required state of facts described in the rule. (State facts 1–2 above):*

_____

_____

_____

_____

Step 4: *Explain why the fact tends to prove or disprove the existence of the required abstract set of facts.(Remember: this step often involves first drawing factual inferences and then connecting the factual inferences to the rule's requirements by using a synonym that references the key facts for the key requirement of the rule.)*

(Draw a relevant inference from fact #1 by finishing the following sentence.)

New businesses often select a location that _____.
(*Hint: What makes a business location desirable?*)

(Draw a relevant inference from fact #2 by finishing the following sentence.)

If Larry were to _____, many _____
would be _____. (*Hint: What desirable state of affairs would exist if what Larry said had been the truth?*)

(Link the two inferences to the rule's requirement by using a synonym for the rule's requirement.)

Thus, a _____ in Betty's situation would _____
if she believed _____.

(Draw a conclusion in the language of the key requirement of the rule.)

Accordingly, because a _____ in Betty's situation would consider Larry's plans _____ in deciding whether to buy Purpleacre, the fact misrepresented by Larry, that he planned to _____,
was a material fact.

Congratulations, you have just applied a rule to a set of facts, and, therefore, have demonstrated the ability to perform a skill that is crucial to success in law school, on the bar exam and in law practice!

15-2.3 Larry Landowner was negotiating with Betty Buyer for Betty to buy, for $50,000, Purpleacre, a tract of farmland on which a corn crop is growing. Betty, who owns a chain of ice skating rinks, was planning to use the land to open an ice skating rink. During negotiations, Larry falsely told Betty that the trees on the land were healthy, when, in fact, two of the trees had diseases that could be treated for less than $10. Betty thereafter agreed to buy the land from Larry. Three weeks before the sale was to close, Betty, who planned to remove the trees, discovered the condition of the trees. Betty therefore refused to close the deal. Larry sued Betty for breach of contract. Is the fact that Larry misrepresented material so that Betty would not be likely to be held liable for breach?

Answer: The question is whether the fact misrepresented by Larry was a material fact (**identification of the issue**).

Step 1: *Identify and state the applicable rule of law.*

Step 2: *Identify and list all facts that tend to prove or disprove the required state of facts described in the rule. (Reminder: Here, the required state of facts is that the misrepresented fact be one that a reasonable person in Betty's situation would consider important in deciding whether to purchase Purpleacre.)*

1. *(Hint: Betty's plans for the land)*

2. *(Hint: Betty's plans for the trees)*

(Hint: The fact Larry misrepresented)

Step 3: *State (in writing) one fact or one set of facts that tends to prove or disprove the existence of the required state of facts described in the rule.*

Step 4: *Explain why the fact tends to prove or disprove the existence of the required abstract set of facts.* (Remember: this step often involves first drawing factual inferences and then connecting the factual inferences to the rule's requirements by using a synonym that references the key facts for the key requirement of the rule.)

(Draw a relevant inference from facts #1 and 3 by finishing the following sentence.)

People who plan to open new businesses usually feel _____ about unexpected expenditures under $10 because _____.

(Draw a relevant inference from fact #2–3 by finishing the following sentence.)

Trees that are in good enough health that they can be made _____
by _____ are still _____ to a
person who plans _____.
Here, Betty isn't even _____,
making the problem with the trees _____.

(Link the two inferences to the rule's requirement by using a synonym for the rule's requirement.)

Thus, a _____ in Betty's situation would _____
if she believed _____.

(Draw a conclusion in the language of the key requirement of the rule.)

Accordingly, because a _____ in Betty's situation would consider
the true facts regarding the trees _____ in deciding whether to buy
Purpleacre, the fact misrepresented by Larry, that the trees were _____,
was _____.

15-2.4   Larry Landowner was negotiating with Betty Buyer for Betty to buy, for $50,000, Purpleacre, a tract of farmland on which a corn crop is growing. Betty, who owns a chain of ice skating rinks, was planning to use the land to open an ice skating rink. During negotiations, Larry falsely told Betty that he always had used the land only for farming. Betty thereafter agreed to buy the land from Larry. Three weeks before the sale was to close, Betty discovered that Larry had, for several years, rented out the land to campers. (The campers, however, never had harmed the land in any way.) Betty therefore refused to close the deal. Larry sued Betty for breach of contract. Is the fact that Larry misrepresented material so that Betty would not be likely to be held liable for breach?

Answer: The question is whether the fact misrepresented by Larry was a material fact (**identification of issue**).

Step 1: Identify and state the applicable rule of law.

_____

_____

_____

Step 2: *Identify and list all facts that tend to prove or disprove the required state of facts described in the rule.*

1. _____

_____

2. _____

3. _____

Step 3: *State (in writing) one fact or one set of facts that tends to prove or disprove the existence of the required state of facts described in the rule.*

Step 4: *Explain why the fact tends to prove or disprove the existence of the required abstract set of facts.* (Remember: this step often involves first drawing factual inferences and then connecting the factual inferences to the rule's requirements by using a synonym that references the key facts for the key requirement of the rule.)

(Draw a relevant inference from facts #1–2.)

(Draw a relevant inference from fact #3.)

(Link the two inferences to the rule's requirement by using a synonym for the rule's requirement.)

Thus, a _____ in Betty's situation would _____
if she believed _____.

(Draw a conclusion in the language of the key requirement of the rule.)

Accordingly, because a _____ in Betty's situation would consider the true
facts regarding _____ in deciding whether to buy Purpleacre, the fact
misrepresented by Larry, that _____
was _____.

15-2.5 Larry Landowner was negotiating with Betty Buyer for Betty to buy, for $50,000, Purpleacre, a tract of farmland on which a corn crop is growing. Betty, who owns a chain of ice skating rinks, was planning to use the land to open an ice skating rink. During negotiations, Larry falsely told Betty that he always had used the land only for farming. Betty thereafter agreed to buy the land from Larry. Three weeks before the sale was to close, Betty discovered that Larry had, for several years, poured paint, turpentine and other chemicals into a pond on the property, and the Environmental Protection Agency (the "EPA") had discovered this fact and was planning, within the next six months, to take action against the owner of the land. Betty therefore refused to close the deal. Larry sued Betty for breach of contract. Is the fact that Larry misrepresented material so that Betty would not be likely to be held liable for breach?

Answer: *Write an answer to this hypo in the space identified below. For each sentence in your answer, identify the step it represents (e.g., Step 1, Step 2).*

15-2.6 Larry Landowner was negotiating with Betty Buyer for Betty to buy, for $50,000, Purpleacre, a tract of farmland on which a corn crop is growing. Betty, who owns a chain of ice skating rinks, was planning to use the land to open an ice skating rink. During negotiations, Larry falsely told Betty that he always had used the land only for farming. Betty thereafter agreed to buy the land from Larry. Three weeks before the sale was to close, Betty discovered that Larry had, in accordance with the law, buried several hundred large metal containers 20 feet underground on a portion of the property Betty did not intend to use. The containers were not harming the property, and an expert with whom Betty consulted, told Betty that he did not expect the containers to cause any harm to the property. However, the expert also noted that no one could say with certainty the containers would not deteriorate and then begin to harm the land because the particular metal used for the containers had only been in existence for a few years. Betty refused to close the deal. Larry sued Betty for breach of contract. Is the fact that Larry misrepresented material so that Betty would not be likely to be held liable for breach?

Answer: (*Hint: This issue could go either way. See Example 3.*) Write an answer to this hypo in the space identified below. *For each sentence in your answer, identify the step it represents (e.g., Step 1, Step 2).*

Exercise 15-3

This exercise has been designed to introduce you to the skill of applying and distinguishing cases. The skill of applying and distinguishing cases, however, requires hours of practice and lots of feedback; complete mastery of this skill, given the limitations of this workbook, is impossible. Each of the hypotheticals below requires you to apply, distinguish or both apply and distinguish *Parker v. Twentieth Century-Fox Corporation* in Appendix B to the text.

Like Exercise 15-2, the first problem in Exercise 15 (15-3.1) is a hypothetical question followed by a model answer. Your only task is to read the question and the answer. **The model answer includes comments and references to the Four Steps of Applying and Distinguishing Cases.**

For the next two problems, the questions will guide you through the reasoning, and the problems are designed so that the analysis strongly favors one particular conclusion. The next question requires you to supply all of the steps on your own but the analysis again strongly favors one particular conclusion. The last question will require you to supply all of the steps on your own, and the problem does not have a clear answer. Use the "Four Steps of Applying and Distinguishing Cases" (Figure 51) as you work all of these problems.

15-3.1   Jack Nickels was a famous dramatic actor who lived in San Francisco. In 2000, Nickels entered into a contract with GMG to star in a new, one-hour comedy television series set in a hospital. The shows were to be filmed in a Los Angeles studio. Nickels was set to play the role of an emergency room doctor. Under the terms of Nickels' contract with GMG, Nickels was to be paid $2,000,000 for the first season of the show, and GMG had the right to renew the show for each of the next two years at $3,000,000 and $4,000,000 per season respectively. The contract also gave Nickels the right to direct two episodes per season and write one episode each season in the second and third seasons. Two months after making the contract and months before filming of the series had started, GMG informed Nickels that it had decided to cancel the series. However, in its letter informing Nickels of its decision, GMG offered Nickels the lead role in an already-existing, successful series, also set in a hospital. The role also involved playing an emergency room doctor and the show was a drama that regularly had comedic scenes and episodes. The person who had previously played the lead had already decided to leave the show. Under the terms of GMG's offer of this alternative role, Nickels' compensation was set at the same figures as in his original contract. Because the show already had an established team of writers, Nickels was not given the right to write any of the episodes but he was given the right to direct three episodes. The show was filmed in New York City. Nickels rejected this alternative offer and sued GMG for breach of contract. Discuss whether Nickels' rejection of the alternative position could be used to reduce his recovery of damages.

Answer (with comments in bold in parentheses): The question is whether GMG's offer of alternative employment to Nickels was sufficiently similar to Nickels' original contract that his rejection of that offer precludes his recovery of damages for GMG's breach of the original contract (**issue statement**). An employee need not accept an offer of alternative employment if it is "different or inferior"(**rule — the *Parker* court stated a rule**).

On the one hand (**signal of argument on both sides will follow**), plaintiff will argue that, in *Parker v. Twentieth Century-Fox* (**signal that a holding is coming**), the court held that an offer of a role in a dramatic movie to replace a role in a musical film (**Step 1 — key fact in precedent case**) in which plaintiff's creative rights were reduced from acting plus input into directorial selection to just acting (**Step 1 — key fact in precedent case**) and where the filming location was moved from Los Angeles to Australia (**Step 1 — key fact in precedent case**) was inferior because the change in genre did not suit plaintiff's then-current artistic interests (**Step 1 — explanation of why the fact influenced the court's decision**), impaired plaintiff's creative input (**Step 1 — explanation of why the fact influenced the court's decision**) and required plaintiff to film in a less convenient location (**Step 1 — explanation of why the fact influenced the court's decision**). Here, similar to the change from musical to drama in *Parker* that would have required the plaintiff to perform in a genre contrary to her interests (**signal author is about to apply the case**), Nickels is being asked to accept a change from a comedy to a drama that merely includes comedic scenes and episodes (**identification of factual similarity**), contrary to his current interests (**Steps 3–4 — decision whether fact is similar enough and explanation of why**). In fact, this change is even more significant to Nickels than was the change in *Parker* (**signal that author is identifying a factual difference that actually makes the case even more applicable — a very effective persuasive strategy**) because, in making the initial contract, Nickels was trying to enhance himself in the acting field by moving from drama to comedy whereas the plaintiff in *Parker* was only trying to do work within her already-existing field, song-and-dance work (**Steps 3–4 — decision whether fact is similar enough and explanation of why**). Also, as in *Parker*, where the plaintiff's directorial control rights were eliminated in the alternative offer, making the alternative offer less creatively exciting to the plaintiff, the alternative offered to Nickels eliminated Nickels' right to author episodes (**identification of factual similarity**), thereby similarly reducing Nickels' creative rights and interest in the position (**Steps 3–4 — decision whether fact is similar enough and explanation of why**). Finally, just as in *Parker*, filming was moved out of the plaintiff's home state (**identification of factual similarity**), making participation the film less convenient (**Steps 3–4 — decision whether fact is similar enough and explanation of why**).

On the other hand (**signal of argument on other side is starting**), defendant will argue that, in *Parker v. Twentieth Century-Fox* (**signal that a holding is coming**), the court held, for many reasons, that an actress under contract to star in a musical was not required to accept offer of a role in a Western film because the role was was inferior. The court concluded the role was inferior because it was a dramatic role rather than a musical role, (**Step 1 — key fact in precedent case**), because it was a secondary role rather than a starring role, (**Step 1 — key fact in precedent case**) because the actress would have had no directorial control in connection with the Western whereas she would have had directorial control under the contract for the musical role, (**Step 1 — key fact in precedent case**) and because the movie was to be filmed in Australia instead of the actress' hometown, Los Angeles, where the musical was to have been filmed (**Step 1 — key fact in precedent case**). Here, in contrast to the reduction in roles in the *Parker* case (**signal that author is about to distinguish the case**), both roles are lead roles in the respective shows (**Step 2 — identification of factual difference**) and therefore are of equal importance to the shows (**Steps 3–4 — decision whether fact is different enough and explanation of why**). In addition, also unlike in *Parker*, where the genre of the two films was markedly different, both shows involve comedy, are set in hospitals and require plaintiff to play an emergency room doctor (**Step 2 — identification of factual difference**) and therefore are within the same general fields (**Steps 3–4 — decision whether fact is different enough and explanation of why**), and, while the alternative employment in *Parker* would have required the plaintiff there to give up directorial rights, the contract here gives Nickels more, not less directorial rights — three, instead of two episodes (**Step 2 — identification of factual difference**) and therefore more, not less, control of his work environment (**Steps 3–4 — decision whether fact is different enough and explanation of why**). This case also can be distinguished from *Parker* because, unlike in *Parker*, where the change of filming locale was from the plaintiff's home to another continent, the change here was from one large city that was not plaintiff's home (Los Angeles) to another large city that was not plaintiff's home (New York) (**Step 2 — identification of factual difference**) and therefore not significantly less convenient because neither city is Nickels' home city (**Steps 3–4 — decision whether fact is different enough and explanation of why**). In fact, the alternative show offered Nickels was already successful whereas the original offer was in a show that might fail and therefore plaintiff was not assured, under the original contract, of being paid for three seasons (**identification of factual difference**). Consequently, unlike in *Parker*, where the two films offered the plaintiff were equal opportunities in terms of compensation, the compensation in the alternative offered in this case is much more secure, making the alternative offer not merely equal but, in fact, a better offer (**Steps 3–4 — decision whether fact is different enough and explanation of why**).

Because the alternative offer was an offer of a role in the same field, a show with comedic elements in which plaintiff was to play a doctor on a show set in a hospital, and gave plaintiff better directorial rights, and was a more secure position, the offered alternative employment was not inferior. Consequently, more likely than not, a court would conclude the employment was not inferior and therefore could be used to reduce plaintiff's recovery of damages (**conclusion that identifies key reasons for author's prediction**).

15-3.2   Jack Nickels was a famous dramatic actor who lived in San Francisco. In 2000, Nickels entered into a contract with GMG to star in a new, one-hour comedy television series set in a hospital. The shows were to be filmed in a Los Angeles studio. Nickels was set to play the role of an emergency room doctor. Under the terms of Nickels' contract with GMG, Nickels was to be paid $2,000,000 for the first season of the show, and GMG had the right to renew the show for each of the next two years at $3,000,000 and $4,000,000 per season respectively. The contract also gave Nickels the right to direct two episodes per season and write one episode each season in the second and third seasons. Two months after making the contract and months before filming of the series had started, GMG informed Nickels that it had decided to cancel the series. However, in its letter informing Nickels of its decision, GMG offered Nickels the role of co-star in an already-existing, successful musical variety series. The person who had previously been the co-star already had decided to leave the show. Under the terms of GMG's offer of this alternative role, Nickels' compensation was set at the same figures as in his original contract. Because the show already had an established team of writers and directors, Nickels was not given the right to write or direct any of the episodes. The show was filmed in Antarctica. Nickels rejected this alternative offer and sued GMG for breach of contract. Discuss whether Nickels' rejection of the alternative position could be used to reduce plaintiff's recovery of damages.

Answer: The question is whether GMG's offer of alternative employment to Nickels was sufficiently similar to Nickels' original contract that his rejection of that offer precludes his recovery of damages for GMG's breach of the original contract (**issue statement**). An employee need not accept an offer of alternative employment if it is "different or inferior" (**rule — the *Parker* court stated a rule**).

Step 1a: List key facts in the precedent case (*Hint — see holdings above*):

1. (*Type of role*)

2. (*Genre of show*)

3. (*Location of filming*)

4. (*Other contractual rights*)

Step 1b: Explain why each of the listed facts influenced the court's decision.

1. (*Type of role*)

2. (*Genre of show*)

3. (*Location of filming*)

4. (*Other contractual rights*)

Step 2: Identify key facts of precedent and compare to key facts of the hypothetical (in the table below).

Step 3: Decide whether each key fact in the hypo is sufficiently similar to reach the same result or sufficiently different to reach a different result and why in the table below, which I have partially completed for you.

Fact #	Key Precedent Facts	Key Hypo Facts	Similar enough? (yes or no or maybe)	Why or why not?
1	Type of Role (fill in) —		Yes	
2	Genre (fill in) —		Yes	
3	Location (fill in) —		Yes	
4	Other rights (fill in) —		Yes	

Step 4: Use the facts and explanations in the chart to write an analysis.

In *Parker v. Twentieth Century-Fox* (**signal that a holding is coming**), the court held that (*state a holding*)

_____

_____

_____

_____

_____

Here, as in *Parker*, where the court felt that (Identify precedent fact #1)

_____

_____

_____

was important because (Explain why precedent fact #1 influenced the *Parker* court's decision),

the fact that (Identify hypo fact #1)

justifies the court in reaching the same conclusion in this case because (Explain why precedent fact #1 justifies the same conclusion)

Similarly, just as in *Parker*, the court regarded the fact that (identify precedent fact #2)

as important because (explain why precedent fact #2 influenced the *Parker* court's decision),

the fact that (Identify hypo fact #2)

justifies the court in reaching the same conclusion in this case because

(Explain why precedent fact #2 justifies the same conclusion)

Accordingly, because (summarize key points from above)

a court would likely apply *Parker* and conclude the alternative employment was inferior and therefore cannot be used to reduce the amount GMG must pay Nickels in damages.

15-3.3 Jack Nickels was a famous dramatic actor who lived in San Francisco. In 2000, Nickels entered
into a contract with GMG to star in a new, one-hour comedy television series set in a hospital.
The shows were to be filmed in a Los Angeles studio. Nickels was set to play the role of an emergency room doctor. Under the terms of Nickels' contract with GMG, Nickels was to be paid
$2,000,000 for the first season of the show, and GMG had the right to renew the show for each of
the next two years at $3,000,000 and $4,000,000 per season respectively. The contract also gave
Nickels the right to direct two episodes per season and write one episode each season in the second and third seasons. Two months after making the contract and months before filming of the
series had started, GMG informed Nickels that it had decided to cancel the series. However, in its
letter informing Nickels of its decision, GMG offered Nickels the lead role in an already-existing,
successful series, also set in a hospital. The role involved playing a doctor who was a surgeon and
the show was a comedy that also included some dramatic material. The person who had previ-
ously played the lead had already decided to leave the show. Under the terms of GMG's offer of
this alternative role, Nickels' compensation was set at the same figures as in his original contract.
Nickels was given the right to write one episode in each of the first two seasons and to direct three
episodes per season. The show was filmed in Orange County, California. Nickels rejected this alternative offer and sued GMG for breach of contract. Discuss whether Nickels' rejection of the alternative position could be used to reduce plaintiff's recovery of damages.

Answer: The question is whether GMG's offer of alternative employment to Nickels was sufficiently similar to Nickels' original contract that his rejection of that offer precludes his recovery
of damages for GMG's breach of the original contract (**issue statement**). An employee need not
accept an offer of alternative employment if it is "different or inferior" (**rule — the *Parker* court
stated a rule**).

Step 1a: List key facts in the precedent case (*Hint — see holdings above*):

1. (*Type of role*)

2. (*Genre of show*)

3. (*Location of filming*)

4. (*Other contractual rights*)

Step 1b: Explain why each of the listed facts influenced the court's decision.

1. (*Type of role*)

2. (*Genre of show*)

3. (*Location of filming*)

4. (*Other contractual rights*)

Step 2: Identify key facts of precedent and compare to key facts of the hypothetical (in the table below).

Step 3: Decide whether each key fact in the hypo is sufficiently similar to reach the same result or sufficiently different to reach a different result and why (in the table below, which I have partially completed for you).

Fact #	Key Precedent Facts	Key Hypo Facts	Similar enough? (yes or no or maybe)	Why or why not?
1	Type of Role (fill in) —		No	
2	Genre (fill in) —		No	
3	Location (fill in) —		No	
4	Other rights (fill in) —		No	

Step 4: Use the facts and explanations in the chart to write an analysis.

In *Parker v. Twentieth Century-Fox* (**signal that a holding is coming**), the court held that (state a holding)

Here, unlike in *Parker*, where the court felt that (Identify precedent fact #1) was important because (Explain why precedent fact #1 influenced the *Parker* court's decision),

the fact that (Identify hypo fact #1)

justifies the court in reaching the opposite conclusion in this case because (Explain why precedent fact #1 justifies the opposite conclusion)

Similarly, unlike in *Parker*, the court regarded the fact that (identify precedent fact #2)

as important because (Explain why precedent fact #2 influenced the *Parker* court's decision),

the fact that (Identify hypo fact #2)

justifies the court in reaching the opposite conclusion in this case because (Explain why precedent fact #2 justifies the same conclusion)

Accordingly, because (Summarize key points from above),

---

a court would likely distinguish *Parker* and conclude the alternative employment was not inferior and therefore can be used to reduce the amount GMG must pay Nickels in damages.

15-3.4 Jack Nickels was a famous dramatic actor who lived in San Francisco. In 2000, Nickels entered into a contract with GMG to star in a new, one-hour comedy television series set in a hospital. The shows were to be filmed in a Los Angeles studio. Nickels was set to play the role of an emergency room doctor. Under the terms of Nickels' contract with GMG, Nickels was to be paid $2,000,000 for the first season of the show, and GMG had the right to renew the show for each of the next two years at $3,000,000 and $4,000,000 per season respectively. The contract also gave Nickels the right to direct two episodes per season and write one episode each season in the second and third seasons. Two months after making the contract and months before filming of the series had started, GMG informed Nickels that it had decided to cancel the series. However, in its letter informing Nickels of its decision, GMG offered Nickels a role in an already-existing, wildly successful comedy series. Although another actor had the lead role, the part was an excellent one that was coveted by many actors. The person who had previously had the role already had decided to leave the show. Under the terms of GMG's offer of this alternative role, Nickels' compensation was set at the same figures as in his original contract. Nickels was given rights to choose his dressing room and costumes (rights he did not have under the original contract), but he was not given the right to write or direct any of the episodes. The show was filmed in Los Angeles, but in a studio located in an area known for having high crime and severe traffic issues (the location of the studio where Nickels' original show would have been filmed had neither problem). Nickels rejected this alternative offer and sued GMG for breach of contract. Discuss whether Nickels' rejection of the alternative position could be used to reduce plaintiff's recovery of damages.

Answer: (state issue and rule)

Step 1a:

Step1b:

_____

_____

_____

_____

_____

_____

_____

Steps 2–3:

Step 4:

_____

_____

_____

_____

_____

_____

_____

_____

15-3.5 Jack Nickels was a famous dramatic actor who lived in San Francisco. In 2000, Nickels entered into a contract with GMG to star in a new, one-hour comedy television series set in a hospital. The shows were to be filmed in a Los Angeles studio. Nickels was set to play the role of an emergency room doctor. Under the terms of Nickels' contract with GMG, Nickels was to be paid $2,000,000 for the first season of the show, and GMG had the right to renew the show for each of the next two years at $3,000,000 and $4,000,000 per season respectively. The contract also gave Nickels the right to direct two episodes per season and write one episode each season in the second and third seasons. Two months after making the contract and months before filming of the series had started, GMG informed Nickels that it had decided to cancel the series. However, in its letter informing Nickels of its decision, GMG offered Nickels a role in an already-existing, comedy series that was the highest rated show in the country. The part was not designated the "lead role" because the show was an ensemble show, meaning that each of the five key characters (of which Nickels would be one) were considered central to the show. The person who had previously had the role already had decided to leave the show. Under the terms of GMG's offer of this alternative role, Nickels' compensation was set at the same figures as in his original contract. Nickels was given rights to write as many episodes as he was inclined to write, and GMG said it would try to make sure he could direct "several episodes per season" but could not guarantee it. The show was filmed in San Francisco. Nickels rejected this alternative offer and sued GMG for breach of contract. Discuss whether Nickels' rejection of the alternative position could be used to reduce plaintiff's recovery of damages.

Answer: (state issue and rule)

Step 1a:

Step 1b:

Steps 2–3:

Step 4:

Reflection Questions for Chapter 15

1. In what ways is issue spotting similar to something you learned before you went to law school?

2. Think of and describe an example from your own life when you have applied a non-legal rule to a set of facts.

3. Think of an example from your own life when you have applied or distinguished a non-legal precedent to a set of facts.

4.   Why are practice and feedback so crucial to your development of the skills addressed in this chapter?

Exercise 16-1

This exercise focuses on helping you assess your learning from your professor's instructional objectives. *If your professor does not provide students with objectives on a topic-by-topic basis, you cannot do this exercise.* This exercise provides you an opportunity to practice this task in connection with three objectives in one of your courses. Accordingly, please select three objectives from one of the courses you are taking right now.

16-1.1 Objective 1.

Translate the objective into your own words (*What does your professor expect you to know or be able to do?*)

_____

_____

What have you done to learn what this objective requires you to learn?

_____

_____

_____

Have you learned what this objective requires you to learn? ☐ Yes ☐ No

How do you know? (*Discuss how you have performed on any relevant practice tests, CALI exercises, classroom discussions, etc.*)

_____

_____

_____

16-1.2 Objective 2.

Translate the objective into your own words (*What does your professor expect you to know or be able to do?*)

_____

_____

What have you done to learn what this objective requires you to learn?

_____

_____

Have you learned what this objective requires you to learn? ☐ Yes ☐ No

How do you know? (*Discuss how you have performed on any relevant practice tests, CALI exercises, classroom discussions, etc.*)

_____

_____

16-1.3 Objective 3.

Translate the objective into your own words (*What does your professor expect you to know or be able to do?*)

_____

_____

_____

What have you done to learn what this objective requires you to learn?

_____

_____

_____

Have you learned what this objective requires you to learn? ☐ Yes ☐ No

How do you know? (*Discuss how you have performed on any relevant practice tests, CALI exercises, classroom discussions, etc.*)

_____

_____

_____

Exercise 16-2

This exercise focuses in on the recommended approach to learning from examinations addressed both in Chapter 16 and in Chapter 8. Select an exam, legal writing paper or exercise on which you have received feedback and then answer the following questions. Keep in mind that the key to learning in general and to learning from examinations in particular is being open to feedback and to change.

16-2.1   How well did you think you had learned the material before you took the test/quiz/exercise/paper? (Check the item that best describes your perception of the degree to which you have learned.)

☐ Excellence   ☐ Mastery   ☐ Competence   ☐ Approaching competence   ☐ Poor

16-2.2   How well did you do on the test/quiz/exercise/paper? (check the description that best describes your outcome)

☐ Excellence   ☐ Mastery   ☐ Competence   ☐ Approaching competence   ☐ Poor

16-2.3   Given your results on the test/quiz/exercise/paper, how accurately did you self-assess your learning? (check the description that best describes your outcome)

☐ Very accurately   ☐ OK   ☐ Poorly

If you did not check "very accurately" in response to the above question or if you "very accurately" predicted a poor outcome, discuss why your self-assessment was inaccurate or why you predicted a poor outcome.

16-2.4   Given your results, discuss how efficient and effective your learning strategies were.

16-2.5   If you did not perform as well as you would have liked to have performed or if you believe that your learning process, while effective, was inefficient, identify the cause of your performance issue. Below is a checklist of possible causes. Check all that apply.

Possible problems in the forethought phase

☐ Failure to set appropriate goal (you set no goal or set an improper one)

☐ Incorrect assessment of the learning task (you erroneously classified the task)

☐ Failure to invoke self-efficacy (you failed to identify past success in similar learning enterprises)

☐ Failure to develop intrinsic interest in the learning task (you did not determine why you needed to learn the material)

☐ Poor motivational strategy choices (you could not stay motivated)

☐ Poor environmental choices (you made bad location, timing, rest sequence choices)

☐ Poor cognitive strategy choices (your strategy choices proved unsuited to the learning task or you also should have used additional strategies)

Possible problems in the performance phase

☐ Incorrect implementation of strategy choices (you incorrectly used the strategies)

☐ Failure to maintain focused attention (you were unable to focus during implementation)

☐ Failure to self-monitor (you failed to recognize a breakdown in the learning process while it was ongoing)

☐ Insufficient persistence (learning task simply requires multiple learning cycles)

Possible problem in the reflection phase

☐ Failure to pursue opportunities for self-assessment (you did not take advantage of or create opportunities for practice and feedback)

16-2.6   How did you do on this assignment (test/quiz/exercise/paper) in comparison to assignments you did before law school?

_____

_____

_____

How did you do on this assignment in comparison to other assignments you have had in law school? Why did you do better or worse on this assignment?

_____

_____

_____

_____

16-2.7 What is the most common feedback you received from your professor on this assignment (or, if possible, on all your law school assignments)?

What did your professor(s) mean by this feedback?

16-2.8 What was your most common error on this assignment (or on all your law school assignments)?

16-2.9 Based on your outcome and your response to Questions 16-2.6 to 16-2.8, how do you feel about yourself and your law studies and why do you feel that way?

If you feel, upset, stressed, or depressed, how will you deal with your feelings in a constructive way? (Consider all of the suggestions for reducing stress in Chapter 16)

16-2.10 Based on your outcome and your response to Questions 16-2.6 to 16-2.8, how will you change your approach to studying similar material in the future?

Exercise 16-3

This exercise is an attempt to cause you to write practice examinations. The best way for students to prepare for examinations is to write practice examinations, obtain feedback on those practice exams and learn from that feedback. In fact, prior to your first set of examinations, you should write at least three practices exams in each subject area (regardless of whether you feel comfortable with your success in learning the course material). Accordingly, find and write out complete answers to at least three essay questions in each of your first semester courses. As you finish each essay, find a way to get feedback on your performance (from your professor, from an honest peer or based on your own self-evaluation), using the questions in Exercise 16-2 to help you learn from that feedback. See Chapters 15 and 16 for lists of sources of past examination questions.

Exercise 16-5

The goal of this exercise is to make sure you have planned strategies for dealing with exam stress. Before taking your first law school examination, answer each of the questions below (except the questions in Question 16-5.4, which you should wait and answer immediately after your first examination).

16-5.1 During the week before the examination, you will do the following activities to help you avoid experiencing exam stress on the day of the exam:

_____

_____

_____

_____

16-5.2 On the day of the exam, you will do the following:

Recall the following past success:

_____

_____

_____

_____

_____

_____

Reframe your concerns about your test results by instead focusing on:

_____

_____

_____

_____

_____

Have in mind the following systematic guides to make sure you do what you should be doing on the examination:

_____

_____

_____

_____

161

Remember that the following things in your life are more important to you than your grades:

_____

_____

_____

_____

_____

Use the following relaxation technique (see Chapter 16):

_____

_____

_____

_____

_____

_____

Try the following techniques if you find yourself stuck while taking the examination:

_____

_____

_____

_____

_____

_____

_____

Reflection Questions for Chapter 16

1. Why do the behaviors designated "the negatives" in this chapter interfere with student learning and success?

2. Have you ever planned how you will prepare for an examination? Describe what you did.

3. Why do expert law students self-assess their learning?

4.   Why do expert law students take practice exams? Why do novice learners avoid them?

5.   Compare the strategies you have used in the past to deal with exam stress and the strategies described in this chapter. Which of the strategies in this chapter might work for you? Which might not?

Reflection Questions for Chapter 17
(For the significant others of law students)

1. Why did the law student in your life decide to go to law school?

2. Why do you want the law student in your life to go to law school?

3.   What are your normal expectations of the law student in your life in terms of daily chores, emotional support, time with you in person, phone calls to you, income, etc.? Which of these expectations are you willing to give up to support the law student in your life?

4.   What are you willing to do to support the law student in your life?